SCHOOL
SURVIVAL

D0599954

SCHOOL SURVIVAL

A guidebook for coping with life and changing school

Louise and Catherine House

Special Topic: Friendship

CF4•K

ISBN 978-1-84550-353-6
Published by Christian Focus Publications
Geanies House, Fearn, Tain, Ross-shire,
IV20 1TW, Scotland, U.K.
www.christianfocus.com
email: info@christianfocus.com
Cover design by Daniel van Straaten
Illustrations by Tim Charnick

Scripture verses are taken from the following versions
HOLY BIBLE, NEW INTERNATIONAL VERSION Copyright © 1973, 1978, 1984
International Bible Society. Used by permission of Zondervan Bible Publishers.

CONTEMPORARY ENGLISH VERSION Scripture quotations marked (CEV) are
from the Contemporary English Version Copyright © 1991, 1992, 1995
American Bible Society, Used by Permission.

YOUTH BIBLE New Century Version (Anglicised Edition) copyright @ 1993
by Thomas Nelson Publishing , Inc., 501 Nelson Place, P.O. Box 141000,
Nashville, TN 37214-1000, USA.

Printed and bound by CPD, Wales

The authors and publishers would like to thank the following for permission
to reproduce their material:

Tom Krause for his poem "Finding your heart".

Agnes Priddle for the dialogues "Talking about God" and "The black eye".

Susanna for stories and advice about playground problems

and for her prayer "Words are great".

The authors used the following material for inspiration:

The Parenting Puzzle by Candida Hunt

for ideas about being a good listener

www.childline.org.uk for help with boys and their problems

Dedicated to our friends in Zimbabwe, who welcomed us and made us feel at home

WELCOME
LOOK OUT FOR

WELCOME

Friends are great – we can't live without them! However, sometimes it feels as if friendships just make life more difficult. Getting on with people is a challenge. This book has been written to help you think about those challenges.

Louise came up with the idea for this book when she was ten years old. Catherine, her mother, agreed to help her write it. We finally sat down to write this book two years later. Many of the stories and diary entries are based on things that have happened in our own family. Many thanks to the other people who helped us including Tom, Susanna and Agnes.

This book is not just for reading - you will also find quizzes and other activities. Answers are on the last pages.

Finally, in this book you will find some words and stories from the Bible. The Bible is our guide book for life. Whatever our problems, we can turn to God's word for advice and encouragement.

We hope you enjoy reading our book as much as we have enjoyed writing it.

Louise and Catherine

LOOK OUT FOR

Zoe and Zac

Look out for Zoe and Zac and their Dear Diary entries.

Activities

Whenever you see this symbol you'll find something to do such as questionnaires, word searches and codes to get your teeth into.

Listen up!

Whenever you see this symbol there's something you need to pay attention to or you're into a new Topic.

Look it up!

Whenever you see this symbol there's something you need to look up in the Bible.

Think about it

Whenever you see this symbol there's something you need to think over.

STARTING

A NEW SCHOOL

Dear Diary, Today was my first day at my new school. My teacher, Mrs North, introduced me and everyone stared. I felt really embarrassed until, thankfully, this guy called Steve said I could sit with him. He's pretty cool and made me feel really welcome. First lesson was PE.
We're doing athletics! Great! It took my mind off everything. Talk Later. Zac.

Listen up

Everybody has to start a new school sometime. For most young people the biggest challenge is moving up to secondary school. This can be an exciting time, as it is an experience you share with your friends. You are growing up and are gaining more independence. Changing schools is part of that process.

Sometimes, however, you have to change schools for other reasons and find that you are the "new" person in the class. It can be difficult making friends when groups have already formed.

However, that feeling of being "new" does go away and new friendships will start to develop.

Dear Diary, My mum had been trying to sell our house for a long time. When it was eventually sold, I had already been in secondary school for over a year. I had settled in and made friends. I didn't want to move. In my first week at my new school I was really surprised at how friendly everyone was. I soon began to make new friends. I still miss my old friends but I get to see them sometimes in the holidays. Bye 4 now. Zac.

LISTEN UP

Changes happen in our lives, like moving schools. It may be difficult, but we know God is always there for us. God never changes - he is always looking out for us and has a purpose for our lives.

LOOK IT UP

"I know what I am planning for you," says the Lord. *"I have good plans for you, not plans to hurt you. I will give you hope and a good future."* Jeremiah 29: 11 (The Youth Bible)

THINK ABOUT IT

When a new person joins your class, club or church, do you welcome them?

QUESTIONNAIRE

Who's your best friend?

How long have you known them?

Where did you meet them?

Who are your friends at church?

What do you like doing best with your mates?

Describe one problem that you are facing with your friend/s.

Who do you talk to when you are having problems?

Complete this sentence: A good friend is someone who…

survival Tips

Here are some ways to help you survive moving up to secondary school or starting a new school.

Be Prepared

- Get all the equipment and uniform you need before you start.

- Keep a copy of your timetable with you.

- Try not to be late for school.

- Don't let homework pile up – get it out of the way as soon as possible so that you can relax.

Be Friendly

- Talk to different people in class – not just your old mates.

- Invite people who are alone to be in your group.

- Go to clubs and out of school activities – they will help you to make new friends.

- Some schools have Christian clubs – don't be afraid to go along.

Get Help

- Remember that your form tutor or teacher is there to help you with any problems you may have.

- Talk to your parents, carers, sisters or brothers about what's going on in your life and if you have any problems.

Trust God

- Trust in God. He will help you.

- Pray. Tell God about what's happening in your life. He wants to help.

Unjumble the words below to find out about true friendship. If you get stuck, look up 1 Corinthians 13: 4–7 in a Bible.

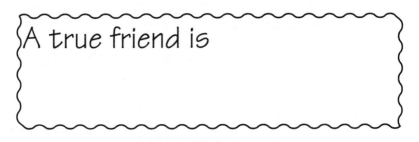

A true friend is

A true friend is not......

atnetip	frttluhu
veuinso	urdop
idnk	lsesefsl
abutofsl	ured

EVERYONE IS DIFFERENT

 It is easy to make friends with people who are the same as us – who come from the same types of home and backgrounds. But today, many of us live in communities made up of different types of people from different types of backgrounds.

The question is: Do we try to make friends with people who are different from ourselves? Perhaps these people come from a different country, have a different religion or culture. In our schools there are children with different abilities and disabilities. Some children may have problems knowing how to behave properly.

We may look different, dress differently, speak differently, believe different things but underneath we are all the same. We all need friends and we can all be friends.

Jesus was a friend to all sorts of people. Often he was criticised for the type of friends he had. On the next page is an imaginary letter to the High Priest from one of Jesus' enemies. Why do you think Jesus made friends with the types of people described in the letter?

Dear Caiaphas

I'm just writing to keep you updated. Jesus continues to step out of line, I'm afraid. He doesn't care what people think. He has even chosen Matthew as one of his disciples! Yes, Matthew, the tax collector! Or perhaps I should say traitor and Roman sympathiser! Jesus doesn't listen to what people say about him. He visited Matthew in his home and was friendly to all his tax collecting friends. Traitors – the whole bunch of them!

Worse than that, some of his friends are just plain common. Jesus never condemns those women who are real sinners. He knows what they do, but he just tells them to stop doing it and that is that. To me it shows a lack of judgment, hanging out with such people. Don't you agree?

I just don't understand him. Jesus always talks to children, blesses babies, heals the sick. He even touches lepers. How crazy is that?

Hope to see you soon

You Know Who

Looks aren't everything

We often say that everyone is special, and yet we treat some people as if they are not very special at all! We may believe that God cares for everyone, but do we show that by our actions?

Sadly, we often judge people by how they look, what they wear and what they have. When choosing your friends remember that in God's eyes these things are not important. Neither should they be important to us.

There was once a rich man who went into a church. He wore the latest fashions and an expensive ring. "Here's a good seat at the front of the church," the church steward welcomed him.

Then a poor man, dressed in rags, came into the church. This time the steward did not even welcome him. Instead he told him to stand at the back of the church away from everyone else.

LOOK IT UP

In the New Testament, this story is told by James. He says that such behaviour is wrong. We should not show favouritism but instead treat everyone with love. Read about this for yourself: James 2: 1–13

GIVE IT A TRY!

 Friendships grow when we do things together. However, sometimes it is difficult to think of what to do with our friends. This page is here to help you.

Look at the following ideas and circle the things that you could do with your friends. Then get your diary, ring your friends and book a date. Remember to check out your plans with your parents or carer, before you speak with your friends.

Have a Karaoke evening

Play rounders

Go to the church youth group

Play football or cricket in the park

Have a sleepover

Go to the cinema

Bake a cake

Trampoline

Go for a cycle ride

Play badminton in the garden

Plant sunflowers

Make a toy model

Go for a run

Play a board game

Walk a friend's dog

Go for a swim

Water fight

Dodge ball

BBQ TIME

BBQs are great fun in the summer. Why not organise one for your friends? Ask an adult to operate the BBQ. Here are some recipes that are easy to make and taste delicious!

Sticky Sausages:

1. Take 2 packets of chipolata sausages

2. Coat the sausages in 1 tablespoon of honey and 1 tablespoon of dried coriander

3. Cook on the BBQ

Sweet Potato Wedges:

This will go great with the sausages!

1. Peel 700g of sweet potatoes and cut into wedges

2. Mix together: the juice of 1 lemon; 1 tablespoon of sesame seeds; 1 tablespoon of honey; 2 tablespoons of olive oil

3. Coat the sweet potato with the mixture

4. Put on a baking tray and bake for 35 minutes at 200°C.

Chicken Tikka

Ingredients:

- 150g natural yoghurt

- 1 teaspoon ginger

- 2 cloves of garlic (crushed)

- 1 teaspoon mild chilli pepper

- 1 tablespoon ground coriander seed

- ½ teaspoon salt

- Juice of 1 lemon

- 750g chicken breasts (skinned)

Method:

1. Mix all the ingredients in a bowl (except the chicken)

2. Cut the chicken into cubes and cover with the mixture. Leave in the fridge overnight

3. To BBQ the chicken, thread the pieces onto skewers and grill

4. Turn the skewers frequently

5. When cooked, remove the chicken from the skewers

6. Serve with a salad and rice

BIBLE STORY: The Good Samaritan

One of the best known stories in the world is about friendship. It is the story of a man who was a friend to a stranger...

One day a religious leader asked Jesus, "Who is my neighbour?" Jesus answered by telling him a story.

A Jewish man went on a journey. As he was walking along a deserted road, robbers attacked him. They beat him up, took his clothes and stole everything he was carrying. After some time, a priest came by. He looked at the injured traveller but quickly walked past on the other side of the road.

Later that day, another religious man came along. He also saw the injured traveller but passed by without offering any help.

Finally, a Samaritan man arrived. When he saw the injured traveller he felt very sorry for him. The Samaritan wasted no time. He bandaged the man's wounds, put him on his donkey and took him to an inn.

The next day the Samaritan had to leave. So he gave the innkeeper his own money so that the injured traveller could be looked after.

"Which of these three men was a neighbour to the man who had been robbed?" Jesus asked.

"The man who helped him," the religious leader replied.

"Go and show the same kindness," Jesus said.

LISTEN UP

- When Jesus told this story, Samaritans and Jews hated each other.

- The story teaches us that a neighbour is anyone who needs our help.

- Jesus was teaching us to be a friend to people we would normally ignore or dislike.

THINK ABOUT IT!

Why do you think the priest and the religious man did not help the injured traveller? What do you think you would have done?

questionnaire?

Are you a Good Samaritan?

1 Your friend moves away. Do you....

a) phone to find out how they are?

b) email them?

c) lose their contact details?

2 Someone in your youth group is raising sponsor money for Africa. Do you...

a) give some of your own pocket money?

b) ask your parents to help sponsor him/her?

c) hide?

3 A child is knocked down in front of you. Do you...

a) talk to him and make sure someone phones an ambulance?

b) check that the driver has stopped?

c) walk on past?

4 It's your party. Your younger brother/ sister is hanging around. Do you...

a) invite him/her to join you?

b) say that he/she can have some of the party food?

c) tell him/her not to bother you?

5 Your friend is really worried about the exams. Do you...

a) offer to help him/her do some revision?

b) give him/her details of useful revision websites?

c) tell him/her not to bother to revise?

6 Your friend has to go to hospital. Do you...

a) ring their parents to ask if you can visit?

b) send a card?

c) joke about it?

7 A new kid joins your class. Do you...

a) say hello and show them around the school?

b) smile at them from a distance?

c) ignore them?

8 Your friend has lost their trainers at school. Do you...

a) go with him/her to the lost property?

b) promise to let him/her know if you see the trainers?

c) go to lunch – it's not your problem?

Mainly As

You're a really good friend. You really care and you show it.

Mainly Bs

You're a good friend as long as you don't have to do too much.

Mainly Cs

Could do much better!

The Golden Rule of Friendship

How can I be a good friend? Crack the code to find out the answer. The key is on the next page.

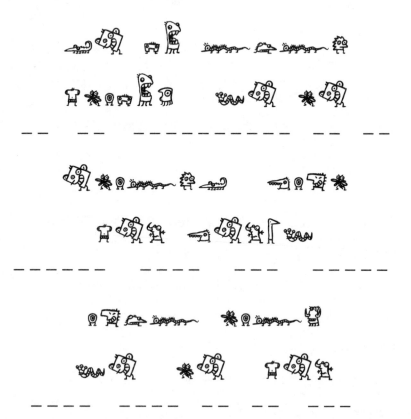

This verse from the Bible is called the "golden rule" because it gives us guidance on how to treat others in a fair and kind way. Jesus taught the "golden rule" (Matthew 7: 12). He also taught people to love God and to love their neighbours as themselves.

a	b	c	d
e	f	g	h
i	j	k	l
m	n	o	p
q	r	s	t
u	v	w	x
y	z		

Dear Diary, Why do friendships have to be so hard? One of my friends has been acting as if she's better than me. I got a few less marks than her in a science test and now she's been boasting and putting me down. It's really hard because I want to shout at her, but my friends know I'm a Christian – I'm supposed to be the one who is kind and forgiving. Zoe.

Listen up!

If the world was perfect and everyone followed the "golden rule" our friendships would be a lot easier. Unfortunately, we often forget this rule or just find it very difficult to put into action. Thankfully, God understands that we find relationships difficult. Help is at hand!

The Holy Spirit:

Gives us strength to live in God's way

The Bible:

Shows us the right way to live

Prayer:

A way to ask God for help

Christian friends:

Encourage us

So can we keep the golden rule of friendship? Yes and No!

NO – it is often too difficult on our own.

YES – when we trust and ask God to give us the strength and courage to be the sort of friends he wants us to be.

When we become a Christian, God gives us his Holy Spirit to help us live a Christian life. We become Christians when we ask Jesus Christ to be our Saviour and friend. We may belong to a Christian family but we all have to make this decision for ourselves. We talk about this more on pages 58–59.

However, things still go wrong in our lives. Sometimes we let our friends down. Other times people treat us in ways that are hurtful. This book looks at some of the problems that happen when we forget to treat people as we would like to be treated.

Word search

Take a break by doing this word search. All the words in the grid are listed below. They describe some things we do with and for our friends. The words may be read across, up, down or diagonally, either backwards or forwards in straight lines.

BBQ	PRAY	CAMP	SHARE	CHAT
SHOPPING	CINEMA	SLEEPOVER	CYCLE	SPORT
DISCUSS	SUPPORT	HELP	TALK	LAUGH
TEXT	LISTEN	UNDERSTAND	MUSIC	VISIT
PARTY	WALK			

T	L	L	V	H	B	T	J	L	V	U	Y	G	P	F
R	A	I	E	K	R	B	A	G	N	U	U	A	D	B
O	C	L	S	O	F	U	G	D	V	I	S	I	T	H
P	P	I	P	T	G	R	E	V	O	P	E	E	L	S
S	J	P	S	H	E	R	C	I	N	E	M	A	C	S
M	U	H	X	U	S	N	H	M	K	K	S	D	Y	U
S	O	A	Q	T	M	I	A	F	L	T	S	L	C	C
K	G	Z	A	H	B	Z	T	A	A	H	E	P	L	S
W	L	N	B	B	Q	F	W	R	T	R	R	E	E	I
X	D	A	I	Y	T	R	A	P	A	D	C	J	S	D
X	T	V	T	P	R	W	F	H	T	A	W	A	L	J
D	C	E	C	G	P	V	S	B	X	O	Y	I	M	G
F	M	W	G	S	W	O	L	G	E	L	P	V	V	P
Y	A	R	P	V	F	V	H	U	T	P	K	U	F	I
J	X	D	E	E	L	W	G	S	Q	Q	B	P	E	O

WHAT IS BULLYING?

 Bullying happens when a person or group tries to upset another person by doing or saying hurtful things. Often people who are bullied are not able to defend themselves easily. When someone is being bullied, they will feel upset, afraid or helpless.

There are many different ways of bullying people. Look at the actions on this page. Circle the ones that are used by bullies. Don't forget to check your answers at the back of the book.

Sharing	Kicking	Threats	Playing
Name calling	Comforting	Ignoring	Chatting
Helping	Encouraging	Whispering	Shouting
Listening	Hitting	Teasing	

Saying nasty things   Ganging up on someone

Going to the shops   Stealing from someone

Texting horrible messages   Damaging property

Bullying Facts

Read the following sentences about bullying. Are they true or false? Go to the back of the book to check your answers.

1. Children always tell an adult when they are being bullied

   TRUE/FALSE

2. Most of the time bullying happens in secret

   TRUE/FALSE

3. Children are most often bullied in the playground
   TRUE/FALSE

4. Parents always know when their children are being bullied

TRUE/FALSE

5. Bullying can cause health problems

TRUE/FALSE

6. Only boys are bullies

TRUE/FALSE

7. The most common form of bullying is name calling

TRUE/FALSE

Think about it!

A bully is always in the wrong. No one deserves to be bullied. If you are being bullied, remember it is not your fault. You have done nothing wrong.

What to do about it

If you are being bullied:

1. Talk to your parents or an adult you can trust.

2. Don't let the bully see how upset you are. Ignore them. Try to be confident.

3. Avoid being on your own. Stick with your friends.

4. Find out about your school bullying policy. It is there to help you.

If you see someone being bullied:

1. Refuse to join in.

2. Fetch an adult straightaway.

3. If you feel safe, talk to the bullies about what they are doing.

4. Speak to the person who is being bullied. Show them that you care.

5. Encourage the person to talk with parents or an adult who can help.

Dear Diary, I had a horrible day. My friends teased me because I go to church. They don't understand. They should just accept it and leave me alone. My dad told me to ignore them. He said that they would soon get bored. But it's so hard not to take any notice. Apart from that my day  was pretty normal. Drama was boring. We spent half of the lesson being told off! P.E. was fun though, we played football and my team won 3-0!!! See you later. Zac.

Listen Up!

Today, many people do not understand why people go to church. You may find that your friends tease you because of your beliefs. Here are some tips:

- Talk to your friends and explain that this teasing hurts you.

- Share your problems with your parents, friends at church or a youth leader.

- Invite your friends to a Christian event that is "youth friendly". They may be very surprised to see other Christian young people having a good time.

- Pray for your friends and ask God to help you.

Break time problems!

These are true stories of people who were bullied at school. Some of these events took place more than twenty years ago. We often remember those who bully us and we also remember those who stand up for us when we are being treated unfairly.

I was bullied on the way home from school. A boy put a stinging nettle in my face. It went into my eye and hurt a lot.

When I went to my new school, Tanaka tried to push me into the mud. Another boy, called William, stood in front of me and told the bully to leave me alone.

One day, when I was walking with my sister an older girl in my school started to hit me. My sister told me to run home and the bully knocked her to the ground.

Think about it!

Will you be remembered as a person who stood up against bullying?

Bullying is Real

My friend, Harry, has a mood problem. He fights with us and gets angry at the slightest thing. Recently he has improved because he says to himself, "If I don't hit anyone or get angry, I won't get into trouble!"

Once I fell out with my friends. I sat in the corner of the playground and they teased me. After a few days we made up, but it still hurt me.

One day in the play ground a girl said that I was calling her names. This was not true but the teacher believed her. Now I try to keep out of her way, because I know she cannot be trusted.

Listen up

Small problems happen just like a little breeze. But when more and more people get involved the little breeze can become a tornado. This happened to me. I got involved in my friend's argument and in the end the teacher called my parents. A little problem became a huge one.

Turn the page to find out about some things that you can do about bullying during break times. You may do different things in different situations. If you are still at primary school, what are your playground rules?

Walk Away

- When someone is being mean, try to ignore them.

- Walk away when people are being nasty.

- Don't let them know that you are upset because then they will get bored and stop.

- If someone calls you a name – ignore it and don't call them names back.

- If someone hits you, don't hit them back because you will also get into trouble.

- When people gang up against you or won't let you join in their games, find someone else to hang out with.

Speak out

- Tell the person that you don't like what they are doing – hopefully they will understand and stop.

- If someone is giving you the silent treatment – tell them that you don't like it.

- If you are having problems during break times – don't be shy about telling other people. Tell your teacher and your parents.

Think before you act

- Don't whisper to some friends because other friends may feel left out.

- If you are having an argument with a friend – FREEZE and COUNT! This means count to 10 in your head because it helps to calm you down.

- Be careful about getting involved in other people's business. Often people who are having an argument need to sort it out for themselves. You might only make things worse.

Think about it!

How can you stop little problems between friends becoming big problems?

BIBLE STORY:
Friends Forever

King Saul was going mad with jealousy, hatred and fear. It was all to do with one young man called David. David was such a hero; the people loved him, the army loved him but most of all God loved him.

So King Saul tried to make life difficult for him. He even threw his spear at David whenever he felt annoyed. Yet David was quick on his feet and managed to jump clear.

"I will send him into battle," King Saul said to himself. "The Philistines will get rid of him for me." But that didn't work either. David was a skilled fighter and constantly won his battles.

Finally, King Saul called his son, Jonathan. "I am so fed up with David. I want you to kill him."

However, Jonathan and David were best friends. Jonathan knew that his father was wrong and so spoke up for his friend. "David is innocent. There is no reason to kill him."

King Saul listened to Jonathan for a while. However, as time went past the King became angry with David again. One night, he sent his guards to David's house in order to kill him.

"You must flee for your life," David's wife begged him. Then she helped him escape through the window. David went to Jonathan to tell him what had happened.

A few days later Jonathan was having dinner with his father.

"Go and get David," the King ordered. "He must die!"

Once again Jonathan refused. The King was furious, "How dare you protect David! I will never let you rule this kingdom." Then King Saul threw his spear at his own son, but missed.

Jonathan went to warn David and helped him to escape. "We will be friends for ever," the two men promised each other.

Today, we remember Jonathan as the man who stood up against King Saul in order to protect his friend. He was brave and challenged his father's behaviour, even though this meant that his own life was in danger. Jonathan was a true friend.

WHEN I AM ALONE

 It happens! We all have those moments when we feel alone, and wonder whether we have any friends at all. Maybe this has happened to you when you went somewhere and didn't know anyone in the room. Perhaps you have felt lonely because you moved house or school and had to start building friendships all over again. Or you may feel lonely because you find it difficult making friends and sometimes feel that you don't quite fit in.

At times like this, we need to remind ourselves that God is closer than any friend and we can trust his promises.

 ## God's Bible promises

1. God will give us strength when we feel weak.

2. God cares for us.

3. Jesus will always be with us.

4. God loves us as his own children

5. Whatever happens to us, God will use it for good.

 Look up the Bible verses on the next page and write them in the boxes. Match the verses with the promises above. Write the number of the promise next to each box.

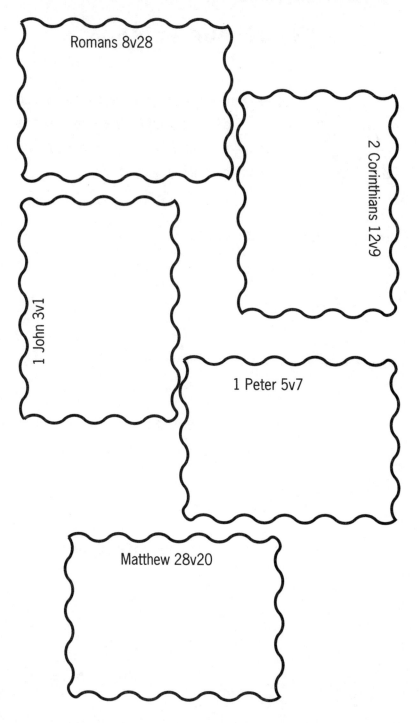

Romans 8v28

2 Corinthians 12v9

1 John 3v1

1 Peter 5v7

Matthew 28v20

Jesus our Friend

It doesn't matter whether we have a best friend or lots of different friends, because Jesus is always there for us and will never let us down. Unmuddle the following sentences:

always to Jesus me listens

me is always He with

Jesus problems our understands

times me encourages when hard are He

answers He prayers my

strength gives He me

lets down me never Jesus

loves Jesus me

Finding your Heart

Do not be afraid, for even now God knows the
yearnings of your heart,

And is sending you His answer to your prayers.

Though you may not know the ways of your journey,

He is guiding you with His gentle touch.

He is perfecting you for a great service,

one that will help others.

Be patient, you are not alone.

For the Lord will hold you in His hands

and protect you.

Someday His plan will become clear to you

And in the end you will find peace.

Until such time walk in faith.

Remember-God loves you.

You are His child.

Written by Tom Krause

Copyright 2000

Word Grid

If you get stuck, look for the answers at the back of the book.

Across:

3.   A person who does or says hurtful things

6.   BBQ food

9.   Another word for verbal bullying

13.   God has a _____ for our lives

15.   A true friend is not _____

16.   Someone to help you at school

18.   A person from the Bible who was a good friend

19.   Someone who is always with us

20.   You should _____ before you act

Down:

1.   A place to meet friends

2.   Something to do with your friends

4.   Tells us the right way to live

5.   Remember God _____ you

7.   When we disagree with our friends

8.   The Holy _____

10.   The good _____

11.   Something we all need

12.   The _____ rule

14.   A way to ask God for help

17.   The Samaritan took the injured man here

STICKS
AND STONES

 We all know the saying, 'Sticks and stones may break my bones but words will never hurt me.' But we also know that this is not true and words do hurt us. Words can be nasty and spiteful. They can damage our friendships.

What we say has a huge impact on our friendships. We can use our words in good or bad ways. However, the Bible warns us that the tongue is difficult to control. (Look up James 3v1-12). Learning to control what we say is something that we have to learn. It takes commitment, effort and inner strength.

The next few pages will look at this whole issue of our friendships and what we say. Are you up to a challenge?

KNOCK DOWN OR BUILD UP

When we talk with our friends, do we use words that make them feel sad and that knock their confidence? Or do we use words that are kind and helpful? These types of words help to build people's confidence. They help our friends to feel good about themselves and the friendship we share.

Look at these sentences. Which of them would upset your friends? Which of these sentences are confidence builders?

What's that on your face? Oh, it's just a spot!

I like your hair cut – it really suits you!

Would you like to come around during the holiday?

Is that all you got in the test?

Nice trainers... NOT!!!

LOOK IT UP

When you talk, do not say harmful things, but say what people need – Words that will help others become stronger. Then what you say will be good to those who listen to you. Ephesians 4:29 (The Youth Bible)

Getting criticised by our friends is part of life but it can make us feel very miserable. However, criticism is an important way of helping us to grow as people. Knowing what to do when we are criticised is part of growing up.

What God says

Listen to advice and accept instruction, and in the end you will be wise. Proverbs 19:20

What can I do when I am criticised?

1. Stop and think – is there any truth in it?

2. If the criticism is unfair, forget it and pray for the person who criticised you.

3. If there is some truth in the criticism, then ask yourself: what can I learn from this?

4. Decide on any actions you can take as a result of the criticism.

5. Sometimes criticism can be fair, but there is nothing we can do about it. If this is the case, talk to someone who can help you or will understand your problem.

Gossip

 Sometimes people can hurt or annoy us and all we feel like doing is hurting them back by spreading rumours and saying mean things about them. This is gossip.

Gossip never stays a secret. It is like a wild fire that spreads quickly and can cause all sorts of harm. It's more than likely that the person you're talking about will find out what you are saying. After they've found out, your friendship could be ruined.

Dear Diary, Some of my friends have been annoying me and I can't stop myself from talking about them to my other friends. I really don't want to gossip, but it's become a habit and it helps me get my anger out. I don't know what to do. Zoe.

 Gossip never solves a problem. If your friend hurts or annoys you, talk to them. It may be difficult, but it is better than shouting or talking behind their backs. Sometimes we find ourselves joining in with gossip, just because we want to be cool and be part of the gang. One way to stop this happening is to think before we speak. Pause for 10 seconds and consider the consequences. How would you feel if your friend said this about you?

Below is a verse from the Bible (Proverbs 16:28) which warns us about gossip. You need to unscramble the tiles to reveal the verse. Write it in the blank tiles.

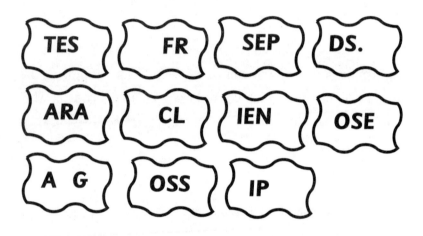

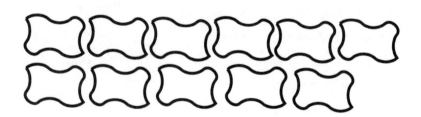

only Joking

Isn't it annoying when someone says something hurtful and then adds "Only joking!" It wasn't really a joke, but you feel that you can't complain because people will think that you don't have a sense of humour.

Laughter is an essential part of friendship but not every joke is funny. What jokes do you share with your friends? Avoid the jokes that are spiteful. You don't need to laugh at jokes that make you feel uncomfortable – be your own person. But here are a few good jokes to get you started.

What did you learn in school today?

Not enough, I have to go back tomorrow!

Why did the elephant cross the road?

Because the chicken was having a day off!

Doctor, Doctor I've got wind! Can you give me something?

Yes - here's a kite!

No Cost

It doesn't cost a thing, to smile and say hello, to ask "how was your weekend?", to explain a difficult homework task, to talk to the new person in the class, to say "well done!", to offer to help to chat to someone without a friend.

It may not cost a thing, but it does require effort. However, when you use your words in a kind and helpful way, people will know that you are a friend they can trust.

What God Says

Look at this Bible verse. Pleasant words are like a honeycomb, making people happy and healthy. Proverbs 16:24 (The Youth Bible)

Think about it

What do you think the Bible verse above means?

TALKING ABOUT GOD

Dear Diary, Today, my youth leader gave us a task. It was to share our faith with our friends. How am I supposed to bring up the subject; none of my friends are Christians? What am I supposed to say? We have to make up our own ideas! But if we're stumped our youth leader will give us some ideas next week. I think I might wait till she gives us the ideas. I don't want to make myself look like an idiot. Zoe x

It's difficult to talk to friends about what we believe. Will they understand? Will they laugh? How do I even start? However, if we ask God to give us opportunities to talk to our friends this will happen! We need to ask God to help us to say something when we get the chance.

There are two ways of sharing our faith:

1. By what we say, 2. By what we do.

If we say we are a Christian but do not act like a Christian, our friends will not take us seriously.

Take a moment to think about your friends and then ask yourself the questions on the following page...

• Do they know you are a Christian?

• How do you try to show them that you follow Jesus?

• What problems do you face when you talk about your faith?

• Where can you go for help about these problems?

Dear Diary, I met up with the church youth group again and I'm not the only one having problems sharing my faith! We wrote down all our ideas, discussed them and chose which ideas were the best. Tomorrow I'm going to invite Hannah to the church youth group. I hope she will come.

HoW 2 TELL oTHERS

• How to tell others that you are a Christian.

• Be yourself and use your own words.

• Don't get angry.

• Don't be rude about other people's beliefs.

• Tell stories from your own life about your faith and beliefs.

• Show by example that you believe what you say.

• Invite your friends to church activities for young people.

• Learn verses and stories from the Bible that will help you explain your faith.

• Pray for your friends and trust God to be working in their lives.

WhaT God says

For God so loved the world that he gave his one and only Son, that whoever believes in him shall not perish but have eternal life. John 3: 16 (NIV)

57

our friendship with God

When my friends ask me about being a Christian, I get a piece of paper and draw the following pictures. They help me explain how you become a Christian. It's not simply about being good.

1) We are made to live in friendship with God

God loves us and wants us to live as part of his family.

2) Our friendship with God is broken

We all do, think or say things that are wrong. These wrong things break our friendship with God. We call this sin. It separates us from God.

3) We cannot repair this friendship for ourselves

People try all sorts of things to reach out to God, such as doing good works. However, we can never be good enough. God has given us his own way to repair our friendship with God....

4) God's way to repair our friendship is through Jesus Christ

God sent his own son, Jesus Christ, to bring us back into friendship with Him. He died on the cross and rose again for us so that our sins can be forgiven. If we trust Jesus as our Saviour and ask him to control our lives, God will forgive the wrong things in our lives. We can then live in friendship with God.

Words are great!

Dear God, Thank you for giving us tongues to speak kind words to people whose spirits are down; words of encouragement, kindness and love.

Words that keep us going no matter what life throws at us.

Words that help us to keep believing in you.

Words that help the sad become happy and the discouraged to see hope in the future.

Words that start a spark in someone's life, that builds up into a huge fire.

Words can change the way someone feels, thinks and acts.

Words are great!

THANK YOU GOD!

Amen

(Written by Susanna aged 11)

Hidden sentence:

— — —   — — — —   — — —

Word search

Complete the word search and find the hidden sentence, which is in the first two lines.

ACTIONS	GOSSIP	ADVICE	HELPFUL
BELIEF	JESUS	CARING	KIND
CONFIDENCE	PRAY	CRITICISM	RISEN
CROSS	SAVIOUR	SIN	FAITH
TRUST	FRIENDSHIP	TRUTHFUL	GOD
WORDS	ENCOURAGEMENT		

T	G	C	O	D	N	L	A	L	O	E	S	V	E	S
Y	N	O	A	E	U	C	M	U	D	C	A	V	U	D
H	V	E	S	R	T	O	H	F	X	N	V	H	L	F
S	E	I	M	I	I	B	G	H	N	E	I	K	Z	G
J	R	L	O	E	E	N	Y	T	K	D	O	K	E	N
G	E	N	P	L	G	A	G	U	P	I	U	D	H	A
B	S	S	I	F	R	A	B	R	J	F	R	B	D	Y
H	N	E	U	P	U	K	R	T	Q	N	G	V	R	C
A	F	Q	P	S	X	L	A	U	H	O	I	M	R	W
C	R	I	T	I	C	I	S	M	O	C	D	O	W	F
T	R	U	S	T	S	V	Q	D	E	C	S	O	A	W
D	W	G	L	W	C	S	P	M	Z	S	N	I	G	O
O	H	P	K	D	S	C	O	S	M	S	T	E	Z	R
L	M	L	C	M	I	I	D	G	L	H	H	W	G	D
K	F	R	I	E	N	D	S	H	I	P	V	A	P	S

Fill in the hidden sentence on the previous page.

Dramatic Action

Characters: Liz; Martin and John
Scene: Three school friends having a conversation.

John: Hey! I just downloaded the whole back-catalogue of Arctic Monkeys. What's the latest thing you've got, Martin?

Martin: Not much recently.

Liz: Have your parents banned you? My parents tried to do that.

Martin: I decided to stop getting stuff from illegal sites. I use iTunes now.

Liz: But that isn't free!

John: Hold on. What's goin' on? You were, like, the download king. What's changed?

Martin: Um...I'm trying to do what's right, that's all...

Liz: That's not all. Come on, Martin, tell us...It's OK...

Martin: Alright. Well, I'm a Christian now, and I want to live like Jesus.

John: Gonna wear sandals? *[Chuckles]* I'm just kiddin'.

Liz: Give it up, John. Wow, Martin! Tell us about it. Like, what do you have to do?

John: I think that all they do is go to church and be nice to people… that's what makes you a Christian.

Martin: Actually, that's not true. You're a Christian if you trust Jesus as your Saviour.

Liz: But you've got to be perfect, right? You can never get in trouble anymore.

Martin: [Laughs] Yeah, like that's ever gonna happen!

Liz: But Christians are supposed to be good.

Martin: Well I still muck up, make mistakes and get cross and am nasty sometimes - ask anyone!

John: So, it doesn't matter if you do stuff wrong?

Martin: Of course it does, but I can tell God I'm sorry.

Liz: But do you try to be good?

Martin: Yes, of course I do, but I can't always get it right. My Youth Leader told me that no one's perfect - only Jesus, and He forgives me. Jesus has made me right with God, once and for all. Truth is, God loves me just the way I am and I don't have to try to make Him like me - He just does! That really encourages me. Reading a couple of my favourite verses from the Bible also gets me refocused on what's important and stops me believing the wrong stuff, like it's too hard, or that God's cross with me.

John: Do you read your Bible every day? Do you read normal books anymore?

Martin: Sometimes I can go for days without picking up my Bible, and sometimes when I do read it I struggle, but if I ask God to help me, it's so worth it! And yes, I'm still reading 'normal' books. I've nearly made it through my cousin's 'Discworld' series. They're pretty old, but really funny.

Liz: What about dinosaurs?!

John: That's a bit random, Liz!

Martin: Yeah!

Liz: You know, what about dinosaurs and evolution and stuff?

John: You don't believe the world was made in seven days, do you, Marv?

Martin: Six days - God rested on the seventh.

John: Whatever. You don't believe it, do you?

Liz: What about dinosaurs, Martin?!

Martin: Woah, hold on people. I'm only a new Christian. I haven't figured it all out yet.

Liz: You don't know? But you must know!

Martin: Why must I know?

Liz: 'Cos.

Martin: Well, I don't.

John: Look, Liz, Marv can't even get through one Maths lesson without asking Miss Lee what she's on about a million times. How's he supposed to know the answer to every single question?

Martin: I'll talk to my Youth Leader about the dinos and let you know what I find out.

Liz: Sure, OK.

John: Hey, I almost forgot. There's gonna be a party at Max's next Saturday - are you coming, Liz?

Liz: Yep, I'm there!

Martin: Hello…am I invited?

John: Didn't think you'd be going to parties anymore…

Martin: Well, yeah - I still wanna do fun stuff! I'm not a weirdo hermit.

Liz: So, you're still gonna hang out with us and Max, then?

Martin: Yeah - I'm not ditching you guys!

John: Better not, Marvy boy!

[John ruffles Martin's hair.]

Liz: Aww - you two are so cute!

John: Whatever!

HELPING FRIENDS WITH PROBLEMS

Dear Diary, Today Hannah wasn't at school, so I phoned her to see if she was ok. I found out that her Nan had died. She had been really close to her Nan and I know she's going to miss her. I didn't know what to say to her. I wish I could help.

Listen up!

You and your friends may be facing all sorts of problems; small problems, large problems, problems that can be solved, problems that will never go away. Perhaps you want to help your friend but their problem is just too big and difficult. What can we do to help someone who is sad because of a death in the family? What can we do when a friend is unhappy due to problems at home?

So often we cannot help as we would like. We cannot make the problems go away. We do not have the right words. We cannot even understand what our friends are going through.

In the next few pages we are going to be looking at what we can do when this happens. Whatever problems our friends face we can always show that we care. There are three things that we can always do to be a good friend.

We can:
- Listen
- Help our friends to find support
- Pray

One way to build friendships is to listen to each other. This may sound easy, but sometimes we are too busy and full of our own lives to listen properly. Look at the following pictures. They show some helpful and less helpful ways of listening.

Unhelpful

Helpful

Tips for being a good listener

1. Look at the person and give your full attention.

2. Keep focused; try not to let your mind wander.

3. Let your friend finish speaking before you say anything.

4. Ask questions.

5. If you are unsure what your friend is trying to say, repeat what you have heard in your own words. This will give your friend the chance to correct you if you have got it wrong.

6. Now and then show that you are listening by nodding or by saying "yeah"

7. Remember that if you don't say anything, your friend will think that you agree with him or her.

8. Don't feel that you always have to give advice. Most of the time, our friends simply want to know that we care enough to listen to them.

What God says

Everyone should be quick to listen, slow to speak and slow to become angry. James 1: 19 (NIV)

Where to get Help

	School Work	Bullying	Health Issues	Racism	Feeling Sad	Problems about sex	Eating problems	Death	Family Break Up	Drink/Drugs	Violence at home
Doctor											
Teachers											
Telephone helplines											
Websites											
School Support Group											
Youth Worker											
Church Leader											
Books											
The Bible											
Parents											

Listen up!

Where can you and your friends get help? The story on the following page shows how a group of men could not change their friend's situation but they knew a man who could! Who do you think that was? Jesus, of course!

Helping our friends find the right sort of support and advice is an important part of being a good friend.

Look at the table on the opposite page. Across the top are places where you can get help. Down the side are different types of problems. Tick the boxes to show where you or your friends could get help when facing these problems.

Bible story:

THE GALILEAN TIMES

Vandals destroy roof

Once again Jesus has been at the centre of a troubling event. Yesterday a group of men vandalised the roof of a house in Capernaum.

"We had no choice. There was such a large crowd of people that we could not get into the house. We wanted to take our friend to see Jesus who was inside. We believed that Jesus would help him," one of the men told reporters.

The men vandalised the roof by making a large hole, so that they could lower their friend down in front of Jesus.

"John has been unable to walk for such a long time.

We had heard that Jesus can heal people.

We didn't want John to miss the chance of meeting him," another one of the vandals explained.

It is reported that when Jesus saw the paralysed man, he healed him. "John is now at home and able to walk," the man's friends confirmed.

Strangely, the owner of the house does not seem to be upset by the state of his roof. "Jesus has come to help people. I am happy that this man is healed," the owner said to reporters.

BOYS' ZONE

Do boys have problems? Of course they do! However, sometimes boys find it harder to talk about these problems. They often think that they should cope on their own. So some boys will not seek help until the problem has become very serious.

Boys and girls face the same sort of problems. However, some boys find it difficult to describe their problem. They talk about other things and find it hard to get to the point.

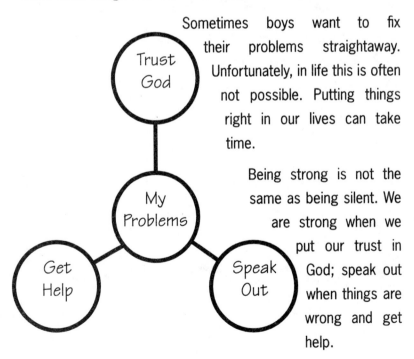

Sometimes boys want to fix their problems straightaway. Unfortunately, in life this is often not possible. Putting things right in our lives can take time.

Being strong is not the same as being silent. We are strong when we put our trust in God; speak out when things are wrong and get help.

73

So what's the point? Simply, if you have friends who are boys, be careful what you say! If you are a boy read the information below – it's for you.

DON'T SAY THINGS LIKE:

· Pull yourself together

· Ignore it – the problem will go away

· Don't cry

· If you have a problem you're just weak

· Grow up – be a man!

DO SAY THINGS LIKE:

· You are not alone – other people have the same problems

· Have you told anyone about this?

· Be yourself – don't compare yourself with others

· It's ok to talk about your problems

CAN YOU HELP?

...re is a quiz about helping your friends. Choose ...e answer from each list. The answers are at ...e back of the book.

...d is being bullied. What do you do?

...e him to talk to an adult.

...e deserves it.

...the bully.

...ur friend has started smoking. What should yo...
...o?

a) Start smoking too.

b) Avoid them.

c) Talk to them about it.

GIRLS' ZONE

 We all have times when we feel bad about ourselves, for example, when things don't go well at school or at home. However, some girls can feel especially bad about themselves because of the way they look.

If you worry about the way you look, remember:

· Everyone is born with a different body and with different looks. God has made you special.

· Growing up can be a difficult time. Our bodies change and our emotions are sometimes difficult to live with. But this is only one stage in our lives and it leads to being an adult.

· Not everything on the TV, in magazines and on the Internet is true. It's not the real world. We should be ourselves, not copy people on the TV.

· True beauty is not about the way we look, it is about our character and the way we live.

· No one feels good all of the time. When you do feel down, talk to someone who cares for you.

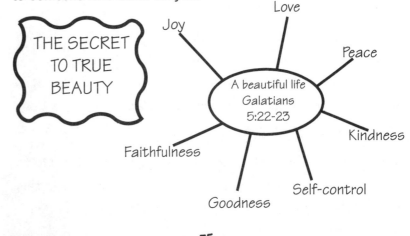

THE SECRET TO TRUE BEAUTY

A beautiful life
Galatians
5:22-23

Love
Joy
Peace
Kindness
Self-control
Goodness
Faithfulness

PRAYING FOR OUR FRIENDS

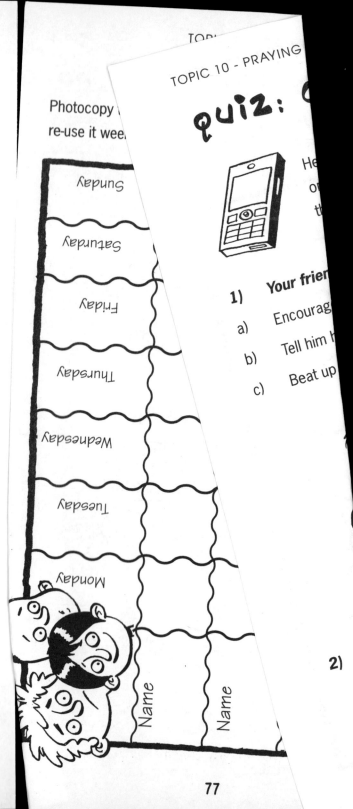

If you want to pray for your friends but don't know what to say here are two prayers you can use - just write or say your friend's name in the blanks.

The first prayer can be used for friends who are Christians. It is based on Ephesians 3: 16-21. The second prayer is for any of your friends.

Dear God, I pray that you will help _____ to be strong through the power of your Holy Spirit. I pray that Jesus will be at the centre of _____'s life. Help _____ to trust you more each day. I pray that _____ will know and understand how much Jesus loves him/her. Fill _____ with your Holy Sprit so that she/he will know that you are working in her/his life. Amen

Dear God, bless _____today. Surround _____with your love and protect him/her with your power. Give _____ strength to face her/his problems and wisdom to know what to do. Thank you for our gift of friendship. Help me to be a good friend to _____. Amen

Try to pray for a friend every day. Here is a diary to help you to do this. Photocopy it several times so that you can have a fresh diary for each week. Don't forget to ask your friends to pray for you.

3) **_Your friend has stopped coming to church. You decide...._**

a) to ring her up to see if she is OK;

b) to do nothing;

c) to talk about it with your other friends.

4) **_Your friend wants to run away from home. What do you NOT do?_**

a) Encourage him to talk to his parents.

b) Listen to why he is so unhappy.

c) Help him to pack

5) **_Your friend has failed a test at school. What do you do?_**

a) Laugh about it.

b) Encourage her to try harder next time.

c) Ignore it.

6) Your friend is feeling down. What advice is NOT helpful?

a) Pull yourself together.

b) Plan a fun day out.

c) Talk to your parents.

7) Your friend is upset because his parents are getting divorced. You decide to pray for him because....

a) God loves him and can help him.

b) You want something to do.

c) It helps you to get to sleep.

8) Your friend thinks that she is useless. Do you...

a) discuss your good points?

b) talk about her good points?

c) agree with her?

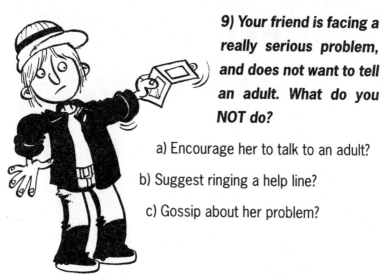

9) Your friend is facing a really serious problem, and does not want to tell an adult. What do you NOT do?

a) Encourage her to talk to an adult?

b) Suggest ringing a help line?

c) Gossip about her problem?

10) Your friend is telling you something important, but there's something on TV you want to watch. What do you do?

a) Forget about the TV programme – it's not important.

b) Make up an excuse that you have to go home.

c) Ask to talk about it later.

WHEN THINGS GO WRONG

Dear Diary, I fell out with Hannah today. Someone told me she hated me. I was so upset I just stopped talking to her. Now she's acting all innocent. She said it was just gossip, but I don't believe her. Got to go, Zoe x

 Friendships do go wrong. We can fall out, say hurtful things or break promises. What do you do when things go wrong? What would you have done if you were Zoe? The next few pages are going to look at two things we can do when our friendships go wrong: saying sorry and being forgiving.

Saying sorry shows that you care and want to put things right, but it is only the first step. We cannot make our friends accept our apologies. Sometimes friends need some space. It can take time for someone to forgive us when we have hurt them.

Think about it!

 When we mess up, God is there to help. We need to tell him what we've done and ask him to forgive us. He will give us the strength to mend our friendships.

82

SAYING SORRY 1

Rachel and Belle were best of friends. They did everything together. Finally the day came when they both went up to secondary school.

"Great, we're in the same form!" they sighed with relief. But somehow things started to go wrong.

The two girls made new friends and started hanging out with them. Small arguments turned into big rows. Rachel and Belle began avoiding each other. Eventually, they didn't even talk.

Weeks passed. Their friendship had ended...or had it? Belle sat looking at her computer. She could see that Rachel was on line. This was her chance. She began to type… hi how r u?

For a few moments there was no reply. Then suddenly Rachel typed back …we need 2 tlk!

The two girls agreed to meet at school. They felt nervous and shy.

"I'm sorry that we fell out." Belle started.

"I'm sorry too. I really missed you," Rachel replied.

"Friends?" Belle asked.

"Friends!" Rachel smiled.

SAYING SORRY 2

Tom and George were good friends outside of school. They lived nearby and helped each other do a paper round. But at school things were very different.

George found school difficult. He was dyslexic and wasn't very good at sports. Sometimes people teased him. The main person who teased him was Billy. Billy was in the 'popular' group and because he teased George, the rest of the group joined in.

Tom was also in the 'popular' group. When his friends teased George he didn't say anything. After a while, Tom also began to laugh at George. One lunchtime, George met up with Tom.

"What's up? You ok?" Tom asked

"Not really. Why were you laughing at me earlier; I thought you were my friend?" George replied.

"Oh, that. I was only joking. You know we're mates," Tom said as George walked away.

However, Tom knew that he had really hurt George, but how could he make it up to his friend?

Later that day Billy, Tom and some of their mates saw George coming out of class. Billy started calling him names.

Suddenly, Tom stepped forward. "Leave him alone," he said.

Billy looked shocked and mumbled "I'll see you tomorrow."

That evening the two boys were doing their paper round. "What made you stand up to Billy?" George asked.

"You're my mate," Tom replied. "I'm sorry I laughed at you at school. I won't do it again."

When we say sorry, we need to mean it. Here are some tips to help do this....

- Don't put it off

- Explain what you are sorry for.

- Show you are really sorry by your actions

- Understand that your friend may find it difficult to forgive you

Remember that there is no easy way to say sorry. It takes strength and courage to say that we have done something wrong. It also takes strength to try not to do the same thing again. We can't do this on our own; we need to ask for God's Spirit to help us.

What God says

The Spirit helps us in our weakness. Romans 8: 26 (NIV)

Think about it!

It's never too late to say sorry.

forgiveness unlimited

Why should I forgive my friends? How many times should I forgive my friend? Surely there comes a point when I should simply dump them?

Jesus told a story to answer these questions. Read the following story and then think about these questions again.

Bible story:
Royal Debts

There was once a king whose servants owed him a lot of money. The day came when the king wanted to collect his money. The first servant to be called owed ten thousand pounds, but he was unable to pay.

"Take him away!" ordered the king. "Sell him and his family as slaves, and then bring me the money."

86

"Please be patient with me!" pleaded the servant. "I will pay you back."

The king looked at the servant and felt sorry for him.

"You can go!" he announced. "I have cancelled your debt."

The servant immediately left the room to tell his family the good news. But on his way, he bumped into another servant, who owed him ten pounds.

"Hey, you!" he shouted and grabbed the man by the neck.

"Where's my money? I want it NOW!"

"It's been a hard month and I don't have a penny. Please be patient, I will pay you back," begged the man.

But the first servant would not listen. Instead he threw the man into prison. "Stay there until you pay me back every penny!"

When the other servants heard what had happened, they were deeply shocked and told the king. The king was furious and called his servant.

"You wicked man! I cancelled all your debt because you begged me to. Why did you not show the same mercy?"

The king was so angry that he threw his servant into prison until he could pay back all the money he owed.

(Read this story for yourself in Matthew 18: 21-35)

Listen up!

Jesus told this story to teach us that we should forgive each other from the heart because God has forgiven us. Jesus said that we should forgive people "seventy-seven times" – which was his way of saying that we should never stop forgiving.

However, Jesus knew that we would find it difficult to keep forgiving people when they hurt us and let us down, so he gave us a special prayer to help us. We all need God's strength to be forgiving people.

Our Father in heaven, hallowed be your name.

Your Kingdom come, your will be done,

on earth as in heaven

Give us today our daily bread.

Forgive us our sins, as we forgive those who sin against us.

Lead us not into temptation, but deliver us from evil.

For the kingdom, the power and the glory are yours.

Now and forever. Amen

questionnaire

Can you answer these questions? The answers are at the back of the book.

1) How long should you hold a grudge?

a) forever b) until your friend says sorry c) as short a time as possible

2) Forgiveness is good for your...

a) bank account b) health c) exam results

Get Well

3) Which of these did Jesus say?

a) Always forgive your enemies – nothing annoys them so much

b) Without forgiveness, there is no future

c) Forgive and you will be forgiven

4) How many words can you make using the letters in the word FORGIVENESS? Write them in the box below:

5) How many times should we forgive our friends? _____

God loves you and has chosen you as his own special people. So be gentle, kind, humble, meek and patient.

Put up with each other, and forgive anyone who does you wrong, just as Christ has forgiven you.

Love is more important than anything else.

It is what ties everything completely together.

Colossians 3:12-14

(Contemporary English Version)

More Dramatic Action

Characters: Tom and Phil
Scene: Phil is chatting with his youth leader.
Phil has a black eye.

Tom: Whoa, how'd you get that black eye?!
Phil: Jasper was telling everyone lies about me and stuff, so I found him and started a fight.
Tom: Jasper?
Phil: Yeah.
Tom: Jasper whose football you slashed?
Phil: Yeah. Well, if he hadn't dropped me from his team, I wouldn't have wrecked his football!...My eye really hurts!
[Laughs]
Tom: I don't think it's funny, Phil.
Phil: I only did to him what he did to me.
Tom: So what's he gonna do back to you?

92

Phil: Well, whatever he does, I'll be ready. My brother's got loads of mates who'll fight – we could take him!

Tom: Then Jasper's brother and his mates will come after you! Can't you see this will go on forever unless you forgive each other?

Phil: Tom, do I look like a loser?! Come on!

Tom: Actually, you have to be strong to forgive.

Phil: No, you don't! Forgiving someone is like giving in.

Tom: Actually, taking revenge and being angry is giving in to the bit inside that wants to be king instead of Jesus. But Christians are supposed to live different. To not let evil get the better of you is really hard. You have to stand up for yourself! It's easy to take revenge, but it takes guts to forgive. Jesus even forgave the people killing Him, while He was dying on the Cross! That's the way He wants us to live, too.

Phil: But Jasper was well nasty to me! I mean, who's gonna sort him out?

Tom: The Bible says you should leave the revenge to God and surprise your enemy with kindness. And remember what Yoda says: *Anger, fear, aggression; the Dark Side of the Force are they.*

CHURCH FRIENDS

Dear Diary, Today Peter came to our class at Junior Church. He must have felt lonely. There were no other boys and six girls! I invited him to our youth group. He wanted to know if there were any boys. I told him there were a few. I hope he comes because he would really enjoy it. Got to go, Zoe.

Look up Hebrew 10: 25 (NIV) and fill in the blanks:

Let us _ _ _ give up

_ _ _ _ _ _ _ together, as

_ _ _ _ are in the _ _ _ _ _ of

doing, but let us

_ _ _ _ _ _ _ _ _ _

one _ _ _ _ _ _ _

Listen up!

It's great to go to church and meet with our friends. However, some young people find that there are few people their age or find it difficult to connect with those that are there. If you are feeling discouraged do not give up, remember...

• friends don't have to be the same age, background or gender as you

• to make an effort to get to know people better – you will be surprised at how interesting they are

• we are all one Christian family – you have an important part to play in that family

• we go to Church to worship God – he understands that you may find this difficult. Ask him to help you.

WHAT"S GOING ON

Going to church or a church youth group can be quite strange if you are not used to. Perhaps you think this yourself! When I invite my friends to something at church, I try to explain to them what is going to happen.

FAQS about church

What's all this singing about?

People sing at church to thank God, to express their feelings to Him and as a type of prayer. Never feel that you have to sing if you don't want to. You can listen and read the words.

Do I have to close my eyes when people pray?

No! But out of respect you could bow your head.

Do I have to wear my best clothes to church?

In most churches you can wear what you want.

Will I have to give any money?

Many churches take a "collection" during the service. You do not have to give to this if you don't want to or don't have any money – no one will mind or even take any notice.

What if I have a question?

Never be afraid to ask. Usually there will be a church leader or youth worker who would be more than happy to answer your questions if your friends can't help.

ON-LINE FRIENDS

 The Internet is an exciting way of keeping in touch with our friends. Sometimes we also use the Internet to make new friends. Have fun, but remember that the Internet has its own dangers. Here are some ideas to help you keep safe.

- Many parents set down "rules" for using the Internet. Remember that such rules are there to help you. If you don't like the rules, discuss them – don't just ignore them.

- Do not give out personal details, such as email addresses, mobile numbers, postal addresses and telephone numbers, to people on the Internet.

- Beware of spam or junk email and texts. Do not believe them or reply to them.

- Do not give people your passwords – not even your friends.

- Do not open files, emails, links or website addresses from people you do not know. These can contain viruses or unpleasant pictures.

- Remember that someone on-line may be lying. If a person wants to meet you in the real world, talk to a parent or carer.

- If something makes you feel uncomfortable, tell an adult straightaway.

Dear Diary, I'm really annoyed. Someone has been on my messenger, claiming to be me, swearing and saying mean things to my mates. I don't know who could have got my password? The only person I've given my password to is my best friend, but she wouldn't have done it. Would she?

Maybe she told someone else? From now on, I'm not going to tell ANYONE my password. Zoe x

Think about it!

How much time do you spend on the internet each week? Could you be doing something else?

Questions and Answers

Q: My parents have rationed the time I'm allowed on the Internet. It's not fair! Why are they doing this to me?

A: It may seem unfair, but they may be worried that you are wasting your time. If you want to spend more time talking to your friends go to visit them. Your parents will be pleased to see you doing more than just sitting at the computer.

Q: My parents won't let me put my picture on my website. I don't understand why?

A: If you put a picture on line, anyone can

take it and use it. Your parents don't want you to give out private information, including what you look like. They just want to protect you.

Q: Sometimes people I don't know get hold of my email and want to chat. What's wrong with that?

A: The problem is that you may think it's just another young person, but it could be an adult pretending to be a child. The best thing to do is to delete them from your address book when you find out you don't know them.

Listen up!

You're almost there – only a few more pages to go. The following questions deal with some of the main points in this book. Write the answers in the spaces provided. Look back through the book to find any answers that you are unsure of or to check your answers. The page numbers are given to you.

1) What is the "golden rule" of friendship? (pages 26–27)

2) How does God help us to be good friends? (page 14)

3) What is the most common form of bullying? (page 33)

4) Write two things you can do if you are being bullied. (page 34)

5) How can God help us when we are lonely? (page 42)

6) Why is gossip a problem? (pages 51–52)

7) How can we help our friends when they are facing difficult problems? (pages 65–67)

8) Write down two things you can do to be a good listener. (page 68)

9) Why should we forgive our friends? (pages 86–89)

10) Write down two things you can do to be safe when using the Internet. (pages 98–100)

TOP TIPS ON FRIENDSHIP

 What are your top tips on friendship? Have a look at the tips on this page and then turn over to page 104 and have a go at making up your own top tips. You can choose some from the list on this page. Chose the ones you think are the most important. But you can also write down your own ideas.

Pray for my friends

Do things together

Be forgiving

Use words that are kind

Be welcoming to new people

Share the good news about Jesus

Don't judge by the outside

Ask God for strength to be a good friend

Treat friends as I would like to be treated

Have fun together

Laugh

Say sorry

Be a good listener

Do not gossip

My top tips!

1) _____

2) _____

3) _____

4) _____

5) _____

6) _____

7) _____

8) _____

9) _____

10)_____

Page 14: Unjumbling - A true friend is patient; selfless; kind; truthful. A true friend is not envious; boastful; rude; proud

Page 26: The golden rule of friendship. So in everything do to others what you would them do to you. Matthew 7:12

Page 30: Wordsearch

T	L	L	V	H	B	I	J	L	V	U	Y	G	P	F
R	A	I	E	K	R	B	A	G	N	U	U	A	D	B
O	G	L	S	O	F	U	G	D	V	I	S	I	T	H
P	P	P	P	T	O	R	E	V	O	P	E	E	L	S
S	J	P	S	H	E	R	G	I	N	E	M	A	G	S
M	U	H	X	U	S	N	H	M	K	K	S	D	Y	U
S	O	A	Q	I	M	I	A	F	I	T	S	L	C	C
K	G	Z	A	H	B	Z	T	A	A	H	E	P	L	S
W	L	N	B	B	Q	F	W	R	T	R	R	E	E	I
X	D	A	I	Y	T	R	A	P	A	D	G	J	S	D
X	T	V	T	R	R	W	F	H	T	A	W	A	L	J
D	C	E	C	G	R	V	S	B	X	O	Y	I	M	G
F	M	W	G	S	W	O	L	G	E	L	P	V	V	P
Y	A	R	P	V	F	V	N	U	T	P	K	U	F	I
J	X	D	E	E	L	W	G	S	Q	Q	B	P	E	O

Page 31 - Kicking; Threats; Name calling; Ignoring; ; Whispering; Shouting; Hitting; Teasing; Saying nasty things; Ganging up on someone; Stealing from someone; Texting horrible messages; Damaging property

Page 32 Bullying Facts/True and False - 1. False 2. False 3. True 4. False 5. True 6. False 7. True. Often children are too scared to report bullying to an adult and most bullying takes place in front of others. Children are most often bullied in the playground. Parents often know when their children are unhappy, but unless the child explains why, they may not realise it is due to bullying. Bullying can lead to physical illness and mental illness. Both boys and girls can be bullies. The most common form of bullying is name calling.

Page 42 - When I am alone - God's Bible Promises
Promise 1 - 2 Corinthians 12:9; Promise 2 - 1 Peter 5:7; Promise 3 - Matthew 28:20; Promise 4 - 1 John 3:1; Promise 5 - Romans 8:28

Page 43 Jesus, our best friend - Jesus always listens to me; He is always with me; Jesus understands our problems; He encourages me when times are hard; He answers my prayers; He gives me strength; Jesus never lets me down; Jesus loves me

Page 46 Word Grid
Across
3 - Bully   6 - Sausage   9 - Teasing   13 - Purpose
15 - Rude   16 - Tutor   18 - Jonathan 19 - Jesus
20 - Think
Down
1 - Club   2 - Cycle   4 - Bible   5 - Loves
7 - Argument   8 - Spirit   10 Samaritan   11 - Friend
12 - Golden   14 - Prayer   17 - Inn
Page 52 A Gossip separates close friends.
Page 61: Word search - Hidden sentence God loves you.

T	G	C	O	D	N	L	A	L	O	E	S	V	E	S
Y	N	O	A	E	U	C	M	U	R	C	A	V	U	D
H	V	E	S	R	T	O	H	F	X	N	V	H	L	F
S	E	I	M	I	I	B	G	H	N	E	L	K	Z	G
J	R	L	O	E	E	N	Y	T	K	D	O	N	E	N
G	E	N	R	L	G	A	G	U	P	I	U	D	H	A
B	S	S	I	F	R	A	B	R	J	F	R	B	D	Y
H	N	E	U	P	U	K	R	T	Q	N	G	V	R	C
A	F	Q	R	S	X	L	A	U	H	O	I	M	R	W
C	R	I	T	I	C	I	S	M	O	C	D	O	W	F
T	R	U	S	T	S	V	Q	D	E	C	S	O	A	W
D	W	G	L	W	C	S	P	M	Z	S	N	I	G	O
O	H	P	K	D	S	C	Q	S	M	S	I	E	Z	R
L	M	L	C	M	I	I	D	G	L	H	H	W	G	D
K	F	R	I	E	N	D	S	H	I	P	V	A	P	S

Page 75: Can you help
1. a
2. c (Sometimes a person starts smoking because they have a problem. Maybe they need a friend to talk to.
3. a (Sometimes we need to encourage our friends to keep going to church or youth group.)
4. c (Running away will just make the problem worse)
5. b (You could find out if there was a reason why she failed. Perhaps you could help her talk to a teacher.)
6. a
7. a
8. b
9. c (When your friends come to you with a problem, they trust you not to tell other people without their permission.)
10. a (Your friends are more important than any TV programme.)

Page 90: Forgiveness Unlimited
1) c
2) b – Forgiving and not being bitter helps your mental health
3) c. Quote a – Oscar Wilde, a famous writer. Quote b – Desmond Tutu, a famous church leader
4) Answers can include: give, sin, gone, fin, fig, no, in, sin, song, five etc
5) 77 times – a number in the Bible that means without end.

Page 94:Church Friends
Hebrews 10:25 Let us not give up meeting together, as some are in the habit of doing, but let us encourage one another

other books by Catherine House

Voices against slavery

Over two hundred years ago slavery was a fact of life – it still is for many people today. Children and young people are smuggled across borders and thrown into a life of captivity and worse. We need to speak out again in the 21st century. Our voices need to be heard.

Here are stories of ten voices that spoke out for freedom. Ten people with one voice – a Christian voice – a voice against slavery.

Voices against Injustice

The people chosen for this book are ordinary people who have made a significant contribution to the improving the lives of others. These stories can be uncomfortable to read and will provoke discussion on moral and social issues. Often there are no easy answers to the social challenges that we face.

Injustice is still around us. Where societies lose their moral moorings they need people of courage and conviction to set a radical and just perspective. Our hope is that through this book you will face these challenges with action and prayer.

Louise House

I came up with the idea for this book when I was eleven years old. We had just returned to England after having lived in Zimbabwe for three years. I realised that schooling in England was different and I would have to adjust. I thought that the book would be helpful and because my mother was an author, I asked if she could help me with my ideas.

I really enjoyed writing the book because it was great seeing it come together. I liked working with my mum and she helped me to think of ideas when I got stuck. We also had a lot of fun. After school I used to spend time every day working in her office. It was hard work but I was so pleased when the book was finished.

Catherine House

It was in Zimbabwe that I first started to write books. When I returned to England, I continued to write educational books mainly for African schools. During this time Louise asked me to help her write a book about friendship. I thought it was a great idea but I was too busy with other projects to help. Louise didn't give up and kept reminding me.

A couple of years later I woke up one morning and suddenly felt that I had to help Louise write her book and I had to do it immediately. For the next few months, Louise and I met every day to work together. We prayed about what we should write. Louise had the final say on everything! She was fantastically dedicated to the task.

Writing a book together was a wonderful experience as we discussed real life problems that she and her sister were facing. We were able to look at what the Bible had to say about friendship and learn together.

When we wrote the book, we did not know if it would ever be published. But we both felt this was something we had to do and we had a tremendous time writing a book together. It strengthened our own friendship and our faith.

CHRISTIAN FOCUS PUBLICATIONS

Christian Focus | Christian Heritage | CF4K | Mentor

Christian Focus Publications publishes books for adults and children under its four main imprints: Christian Focus, Christian Heritage, CF4K and Mentor. Our books reflect that God's word is reliable and Jesus is the way to know him, and live for ever with him.

Our children's publication list includes a Sunday school curriculum that covers pre-school to early teens; puzzle and activity books. We also publish personal and family devotional titles, biographies and inspirational stories that children will love.

If you are looking for quality Bible teaching for children then we have an excellent range of Bible story and age specific theological books.

From pre-school to teenage fiction, we have it covered!

Find us at our web page:
www.christianfocus.com

CF4•K
Because you're never
too young to know Jesus